THE LITTLE
BLACK JOURNAL OF
WINE

• *A Wine Lover's Record Keeper* •

ILLUSTRATED BY KERREN BARBAS

 PETER PAUPER PRESS, INC.
WHITE PLAINS, NEW YORK

*The publisher would like to thank
Ruth Cullen and Elizabeth Poyet for their
contributions to the text of this journal.*

Designed by Heather Zschock

Illustrations copyright © 2004 Kerren Barbas

Visit us at www.peterpauper.com

THE LITTLE
BLACK JOURNAL OF
WINE

• *A Wine Lover's Record Keeper* •

*Wine to me is passion.
It's family and friends.
It's warmth of heart and
generosity of spirit.
Wine is art. It's culture.
It's the essence of
civilization and the
art of living.*

Robert Mondavi,
Harvests of Joy autobiography

CONTENTS

Introduction

Navigating the world of wine is much like traveling, and you, like all savvy wine tasters and travelers, know the value of recording observations and personal reflections in a diary or journal.

Each entry page in this book includes space at the top to record wine data, and space on the lower half of the page to formulate your observations, impressions, and ratings.

Whether you've been tasting wine for decades or have just nosed your first glass, the notes you keep will help you remember where you have been in the world of wine, and where you would like to return.

In time, your wine journal will become a treasured road map that leads you back to your favorite wines, helps you avoid wrong turns, and inspires you to further explore specific regions or varieties.

Cheers!

judging wines

*Anyone who possesses the
basic biological equipment,
in the form of a nose and
palate, can taste wine.*

Tom Stevenson

JUDGING WINES

Observing and recording the particulars of wines you taste will help you develop a sense of your  personal preferences, while helping you differentiate and remember the wines themselves. When judging a wine, consider the style (dry or sweet), intensity (strong or light), aroma (fruity, vegetable, or mineral), acidity (high or low), tannin (astringent, firm, or soft), and texture (smooth or crisp). Observations can be divided into four categories: APPEARANCE, NOSE, TASTE, and FINISH.

APPEARANCE

The visual appearance of a wine—the COLOR, HUE, and LEGS—indicates its body or weight and alcoholic strength. Evaluate the COLOR of the wine by holding up the glass at a 45 degree angle in front of a white background, such as a tablecloth. Remember that flavor is not proportional to intensity of color. But color *is* related to age: red wines get paler as they age, while whites tend to develop a deeper color.

Look for the different HUES in each grape

variety. Chardonnay is golden, compared to the pale, rather greenish yellow of Riesling. Gamay is cherry red, Pinot Noir is a slightly pale vermilion, Zinfandel is purplish, and Cabernet Sauvignon a bluish-black. If a wine looks hazy or bubbly, this indicates problems with fermentation or filtration.

Swirl the wine around the inside of the glass. The dripping lines formed by the wine as it falls back down after swirling are called tears or LEGS. The more legs the wine has, the higher the alcohol content.

In describing a wine's appearance overall, pay attention also to sediment, density, brilliance vs. dullness, and clarity vs. cloudiness.

NOSE

The nose of the wine is its smell. Wine experts used to refer to the bouquet of a wine; now they prefer to say there is raspberry "in the nose." This simply means the wine smells like raspberry.

Assess aroma by swirling the wine again, then putting your nose into the glass and inhaling deeply or in several quick bursts. Inhaling with

 your mouth open a bit can help you smell. Then give your nose a rest for a few moments and try again.

Descriptors of a wine's aroma include a range of imaginative adjectives that fall within these general categories: fruity, spicy, floral, vegetal, chocolate, savory, mineral, and animal.

TASTE

The taste of the wine, as we experience it, is actually composed of four elements: TASTE, AROMA, BODY, and TEXTURE.

The tongue is capable of registering four TASTES: sweetness on its tip, sourness or acidity on the sides, bitterness, such as tannin, at the back, and saltiness (not normally found in wines). Swishing the wine around in your mouth brings it into contact with all the tasting areas on the tongue.

Up to 10,000 other flavors are experienced not by the tongue but by the nasal receptors in the olfactory bulb. Air drawn through the wine into your mouth vaporizes the AROMAS, which float up to the receptors through the retronasal passage. This is why neither food nor wine has much taste when you have a cold: the receptors are blocked and cannot function properly.

BODY is the impression of the weight and size of wine. A wine with full body seems fuller, bigger, heavier in the mouth; it seems to coat your throat like cream. A light-bodied wine slips easily across the palate, like skim milk. A Chardonnay, for example, has fuller body than a Riesling.

Mouthfeel is the textural impression of softness and smoothness, versus firmness, coarseness, or roughness in a wine. Fabric names are sometimes used to describe TEXTURE: smooth as silk, soft as flannel. High acidity in white wines yields hardness, firmness, crispness of texture; high tannin gives similar results in reds. Low levels of these components create softness, which can be excessive. Unfermented sugar and alcohol also yield softness, although very high alcohol content will give a hard edge.

FINISH

Wine leaves a distinct impression on the tongue and mouth after it has been swished, chewed, and swallowed (or spat). A complex

wine brings many different impressions as you drink it. This is another sure sign of quality. Overall balance also affects a wine's finish; better wines generally have a longer finish.

Tasting Tips

When tasting a new wine, decide if it is sweet or dry as soon as it touches the tip of your tongue. Next, consider acidity, the backbone of a white wine's taste. Without sufficient acidity, white wines seem soft, fat, and flabby. With good acidity, whites are crisp or tart. Tannin provides a similar structure to red wines. A red with high tannin is described as astringent, medium tannin as firm, or low tannin as soft.

Consider what family of flavor the wine represents. Is it fruity? Spicy? Herbal? What specific aromas within the family can you identify? Is the wine light, medium, or full-bodied? Is it smooth or hard?

What is the quality of the wine? Does it have any flaws? Is it balanced? Is it too young, or past its prime?

tasting notes

*Wine is the most civilized
thing in the world.*

Ernest Hemingway

Tasting Notes

WINE:

VINTAGE: PRICE:

PRODUCER:

REGION & COUNTRY:

GRAPE VARIETY:

RECOMMENDED BY:

PLACE & DATE BOUGHT:

PLACE & DATE TASTED:

APPEARANCE:

NOSE:

TASTE:

FINISH:

OVERALL IMPRESSION:

OVERALL RATINGS: 70 71 72 73 74 75 76 77 78 79
80 81 82 83 84 85 86 87 88 89 90 91 92 93
94 95 96 97 98 99 100

OVERALL VALUE: ★   ★★   ★★★   ★★★★   ★★★★★

TASTING NOTES

WINE:

VINTAGE: PRICE:

PRODUCER:

REGION & COUNTRY:

GRAPE VARIETY:

RECOMMENDED BY:

PLACE & DATE BOUGHT:

PLACE & DATE TASTED:

APPEARANCE:

NOSE:

TASTE:

FINISH:

OVERALL IMPRESSION:

OVERALL RATINGS: 70 71 72 73 74 75 76 77 78 79
80 81 82 83 84 85 86 87 88 89 90 91 92 93
94 95 96 97 98 99 100

OVERALL VALUE: ★   ★★   ★★★   ★★★★   ★★★★★

TASTING NOTES

WINE:

VINTAGE: PRICE:

PRODUCER:

REGION & COUNTRY:

GRAPE VARIETY:

RECOMMENDED BY:

PLACE & DATE BOUGHT:

PLACE & DATE TASTED:

APPEARANCE:

NOSE:

TASTE:

FINISH:

OVERALL IMPRESSION:

OVERALL RATINGS: 70 71 72 73 74 75 76 77 78 79
80 81 82 83 84 85 86 87 88 89 90 91 92 93
94 95 96 97 98 99 100

OVERALL VALUE: ★   ★★   ★★★   ★★★★   ★★★★★

TASTING NOTES

WINE:

VINTAGE: PRICE:

PRODUCER:

REGION & COUNTRY:

GRAPE VARIETY:

RECOMMENDED BY:

PLACE & DATE BOUGHT:

PLACE & DATE TASTED:

APPEARANCE:

NOSE:

TASTE:

FINISH:

OVERALL IMPRESSION:

OVERALL RATINGS: 70 71 72 73 74 75 76 77 78 79
80 81 82 83 84 85 86 87 88 89 90 91 92 93
94 95 96 97 98 99 100

OVERALL VALUE: ★   ★★   ★★★   ★★★★   ★★★★★

TASTING NOTES

WINE:

VINTAGE: PRICE:

PRODUCER:

REGION & COUNTRY:

GRAPE VARIETY:

RECOMMENDED BY:

PLACE & DATE BOUGHT:

PLACE & DATE TASTED:

APPEARANCE:

NOSE:

TASTE:

FINISH:

OVERALL IMPRESSION:

OVERALL RATINGS: 70 71 72 73 74 75 76 77 78 79
80 81 82 83 84 85 86 87 88 89 90 91 92 93
94 95 96 97 98 99 100

OVERALL VALUE: ★   ★★   ★★★   ★★★★   ★★★★★

TASTING NOTES

WINE:

VINTAGE: PRICE:

PRODUCER:

REGION & COUNTRY:

GRAPE VARIETY:

RECOMMENDED BY:

PLACE & DATE BOUGHT:

PLACE & DATE TASTED:

APPEARANCE:

NOSE:

TASTE:

FINISH:

OVERALL IMPRESSION:

OVERALL RATINGS: 70 71 72 73 74 75 76 77 78 79
80 81 82 83 84 85 86 87 88 89 90 91 92 93
94 95 96 97 98 99 100

OVERALL VALUE: ★   ★★   ★★★   ★★★★   ★★★★★

TASTING NOTES

WINE:

VINTAGE: PRICE:

PRODUCER:

REGION & COUNTRY:

GRAPE VARIETY:

RECOMMENDED BY:

PLACE & DATE BOUGHT:

PLACE & DATE TASTED:

APPEARANCE:

NOSE:

TASTE:

FINISH:

OVERALL IMPRESSION:

OVERALL RATINGS: 70 71 72 73 74 75 76 77 78 79
80 81 82 83 84 85 86 87 88 89 90 91 92 93
94 95 96 97 98 99 100

OVERALL VALUE: ★   ★★   ★★★   ★★★★   ★★★★★

TASTING NOTES

WINE:

VINTAGE: PRICE:

PRODUCER:

REGION & COUNTRY:

GRAPE VARIETY:

RECOMMENDED BY:

PLACE & DATE BOUGHT:

PLACE & DATE TASTED:

APPEARANCE:

NOSE:

TASTE:

FINISH:

OVERALL IMPRESSION:

OVERALL RATINGS: 70 71 72 73 74 75 76 77 78 79
80 81 82 83 84 85 86 87 88 89 90 91 92 93
94 95 96 97 98 99 100

OVERALL VALUE: ★   ★★   ★★★   ★★★★   ★★★★★

TASTING NOTES

WINE:

VINTAGE: PRICE:

PRODUCER:

REGION & COUNTRY:

GRAPE VARIETY:

RECOMMENDED BY:

PLACE & DATE BOUGHT:

PLACE & DATE TASTED:

APPEARANCE:

NOSE:

TASTE:

FINISH:

OVERALL IMPRESSION:

OVERALL RATINGS: 70 71 72 73 74 75 76 77 78 79
80 81 82 83 84 85 86 87 88 89 90 91 92 93
94 95 96 97 98 99 100

OVERALL VALUE: ★   ★★   ★★★   ★★★★   ★★★★★

TASTING NOTES

WINE:

VINTAGE: PRICE:

PRODUCER:

REGION & COUNTRY:

GRAPE VARIETY:

RECOMMENDED BY:

PLACE & DATE BOUGHT:

PLACE & DATE TASTED:

APPEARANCE:

NOSE:

TASTE:

FINISH:

OVERALL IMPRESSION:

OVERALL RATINGS: 70 71 72 73 74 75 76 77 78 79
80 81 82 83 84 85 86 87 88 89 90 91 92 93
94 95 96 97 98 99 100

OVERALL VALUE: ★   ★★   ★★★   ★★★★   ★★★★★

TASTING NOTES

WINE:

VINTAGE: PRICE:

PRODUCER:

REGION & COUNTRY:

GRAPE VARIETY:

RECOMMENDED BY:

PLACE & DATE BOUGHT:

PLACE & DATE TASTED:

APPEARANCE:

NOSE:

TASTE:

FINISH:

OVERALL IMPRESSION:

OVERALL RATINGS: 70 71 72 73 74 75 76 77 78 79
80 81 82 83 84 85 86 87 88 89 90 91 92 93
94 95 96 97 98 99 100

OVERALL VALUE: ★   ★★   ★★★   ★★★★   ★★★★★

TASTING NOTES

WINE:

VINTAGE: PRICE:

PRODUCER:

REGION & COUNTRY:

GRAPE VARIETY:

RECOMMENDED BY:

PLACE & DATE BOUGHT:

PLACE & DATE TASTED:

APPEARANCE:

NOSE:

TASTE:

FINISH:

OVERALL IMPRESSION:

OVERALL RATINGS: 70 71 72 73 74 75 76 77 78 79
80 81 82 83 84 85 86 87 88 89 90 91 92 93
94 95 96 97 98 99 100

OVERALL VALUE: ★   ★★   ★★★   ★★★★   ★★★★★

TASTING NOTES

WINE:

VINTAGE: PRICE:

PRODUCER:

REGION & COUNTRY:

GRAPE VARIETY:

RECOMMENDED BY:

PLACE & DATE BOUGHT:

PLACE & DATE TASTED:

APPEARANCE:

NOSE:

TASTE:

FINISH:

OVERALL IMPRESSION:

OVERALL RATINGS: 70 71 72 73 74 75 76 77 78 79
80 81 82 83 84 85 86 87 88 89 90 91 92 93
94 95 96 97 98 99 100

OVERALL VALUE: ★   ★★   ★★★   ★★★★   ★★★★★

TASTING NOTES

WINE:

VINTAGE: PRICE:

PRODUCER:

REGION & COUNTRY:

GRAPE VARIETY:

RECOMMENDED BY:

PLACE & DATE BOUGHT:

PLACE & DATE TASTED:

APPEARANCE:

NOSE:

TASTE:

FINISH:

OVERALL IMPRESSION:

OVERALL RATINGS: 70 71 72 73 74 75 76 77 78 79
80 81 82 83 84 85 86 87 88 89 90 91 92 93
94 95 96 97 98 99 100

OVERALL VALUE: ★   ★★   ★★★   ★★★★   ★★★★★

TASTING NOTES

WINE:

VINTAGE: PRICE:

PRODUCER:

REGION & COUNTRY:

GRAPE VARIETY:

RECOMMENDED BY:

PLACE & DATE BOUGHT:

PLACE & DATE TASTED:

APPEARANCE:

NOSE:

TASTE:

FINISH:

OVERALL IMPRESSION:

OVERALL RATINGS: 70 71 72 73 74 75 76 77 78 79
80 81 82 83 84 85 86 87 88 89 90 91 92 93
94 95 96 97 98 99 100

OVERALL VALUE: ★   ★★   ★★★   ★★★★   ★★★★★

*Wine brings to light
the hidden
secrets of the soul.*

Horace

❖

*One not only drinks wine,
one smells it, observes it,
tastes it, sips it, and
one talks about it.*

King Edward VII

TASTING NOTES

WINE:

VINTAGE: PRICE:

PRODUCER:

REGION & COUNTRY:

GRAPE VARIETY:

RECOMMENDED BY:

PLACE & DATE BOUGHT:

PLACE & DATE TASTED:

APPEARANCE:

NOSE:

TASTE:

FINISH:

OVERALL IMPRESSION:

OVERALL RATINGS: 70 71 72 73 74 75 76 77 78 79
80 81 82 83 84 85 86 87 88 89 90 91 92 93
94 95 96 97 98 99 100

OVERALL VALUE: ★   ★★   ★★★   ★★★★   ★★★★★

TASTING NOTES

WINE:

VINTAGE: PRICE:

PRODUCER:

REGION & COUNTRY:

GRAPE VARIETY:

RECOMMENDED BY:

PLACE & DATE BOUGHT:

PLACE & DATE TASTED:

APPEARANCE:

NOSE:

TASTE:

FINISH:

OVERALL IMPRESSION:

OVERALL RATINGS: 70 71 72 73 74 75 76 77 78 79
80 81 82 83 84 85 86 87 88 89 90 91 92 93
94 95 96 97 98 99 100

OVERALL VALUE: ★   ★★   ★★★   ★★★★   ★★★★★

TASTING NOTES

WINE:

VINTAGE: PRICE:

PRODUCER:

REGION & COUNTRY:

GRAPE VARIETY:

RECOMMENDED BY:

PLACE & DATE BOUGHT:

PLACE & DATE TASTED:

APPEARANCE:

NOSE:

TASTE:

FINISH:

OVERALL IMPRESSION:

OVERALL RATINGS: 70 71 72 73 74 75 76 77 78 79
80 81 82 83 84 85 86 87 88 89 90 91 92 93
94 95 96 97 98 99 100

OVERALL VALUE: ★   ★★   ★★★   ★★★★   ★★★★★

TASTING NOTES

WINE:

VINTAGE: PRICE:

PRODUCER:

REGION & COUNTRY:

GRAPE VARIETY:

RECOMMENDED BY:

PLACE & DATE BOUGHT:

PLACE & DATE TASTED:

APPEARANCE:

NOSE:

TASTE:

FINISH:

OVERALL IMPRESSION:

OVERALL RATINGS: 70 71 72 73 74 75 76 77 78 79
80 81 82 83 84 85 86 87 88 89 90 91 92 93
94 95 96 97 98 99 100

OVERALL VALUE: ★   ★★   ★★★   ★★★★   ★★★★★

TASTING NOTES

WINE:

VINTAGE: PRICE:

PRODUCER:

REGION & COUNTRY:

GRAPE VARIETY:

RECOMMENDED BY:

PLACE & DATE BOUGHT:

PLACE & DATE TASTED:

APPEARANCE:

NOSE:

TASTE:

FINISH:

OVERALL IMPRESSION:

OVERALL RATINGS: 70 71 72 73 74 75 76 77 78 79
80 81 82 83 84 85 86 87 88 89 90 91 92 93
94 95 96 97 98 99 100

OVERALL VALUE: ★   ★★   ★★★   ★★★★   ★★★★★

TASTING NOTES

WINE:

VINTAGE: PRICE:

PRODUCER:

REGION & COUNTRY:

GRAPE VARIETY:

RECOMMENDED BY:

PLACE & DATE BOUGHT:

PLACE & DATE TASTED:

APPEARANCE:

NOSE:

TASTE:

FINISH:

OVERALL IMPRESSION:

OVERALL RATINGS: 70 71 72 73 74 75 76 77 78 79
80 81 82 83 84 85 86 87 88 89 90 91 92 93
94 95 96 97 98 99 100

OVERALL VALUE: ★   ★★   ★★★   ★★★★   ★★★★★

TASTING NOTES

WINE:

VINTAGE: PRICE:

PRODUCER:

REGION & COUNTRY:

GRAPE VARIETY:

RECOMMENDED BY:

PLACE & DATE BOUGHT:

PLACE & DATE TASTED:

APPEARANCE:

NOSE:

TASTE:

FINISH:

OVERALL IMPRESSION:

OVERALL RATINGS: 70 71 72 73 74 75 76 77 78 79
80 81 82 83 84 85 86 87 88 89 90 91 92 93
94 95 96 97 98 99 100

OVERALL VALUE: ★   ★★   ★★★   ★★★★   ★★★★★

TASTING NOTES

WINE:

VINTAGE: PRICE:

PRODUCER:

REGION & COUNTRY:

GRAPE VARIETY:

RECOMMENDED BY:

PLACE & DATE BOUGHT:

PLACE & DATE TASTED:

APPEARANCE:

NOSE:

TASTE:

FINISH:

OVERALL IMPRESSION:

OVERALL RATINGS: 70 71 72 73 74 75 76 77 78 79
80 81 82 83 84 85 86 87 88 89 90 91 92 93
94 95 96 97 98 99 100

OVERALL VALUE: ★   ★★   ★★★   ★★★★   ★★★★★

TASTING NOTES

WINE:

VINTAGE: PRICE:

PRODUCER:

REGION & COUNTRY:

GRAPE VARIETY:

RECOMMENDED BY:

PLACE & DATE BOUGHT:

PLACE & DATE TASTED:

APPEARANCE:

NOSE:

TASTE:

FINISH:

OVERALL IMPRESSION:

OVERALL RATINGS: 70 71 72 73 74 75 76 77 78 79
80 81 82 83 84 85 86 87 88 89 90 91 92 93
94 95 96 97 98 99 100

OVERALL VALUE: ★   ★★   ★★★   ★★★★   ★★★★★

TASTING NOTES

WINE:

VINTAGE: PRICE:

PRODUCER:

REGION & COUNTRY:

GRAPE VARIETY:

RECOMMENDED BY:

PLACE & DATE BOUGHT:

PLACE & DATE TASTED:

APPEARANCE:

NOSE:

TASTE:

FINISH:

OVERALL IMPRESSION:

OVERALL RATINGS: 70 71 72 73 74 75 76 77 78 79
80 81 82 83 84 85 86 87 88 89 90 91 92 93
94 95 96 97 98 99 100

OVERALL VALUE: ★   ★★   ★★★   ★★★★   ★★★★★

TASTING NOTES

WINE:

VINTAGE: PRICE:

PRODUCER:

REGION & COUNTRY:

GRAPE VARIETY:

RECOMMENDED BY:

PLACE & DATE BOUGHT:

PLACE & DATE TASTED:

APPEARANCE:

NOSE:

TASTE:

FINISH:

OVERALL IMPRESSION:

OVERALL RATINGS: 70 71 72 73 74 75 76 77 78 79
80 81 82 83 84 85 86 87 88 89 90 91 92 93
94 95 96 97 98 99 100

OVERALL VALUE: ★   ★★   ★★★   ★★★★   ★★★★★

TASTING NOTES

WINE:

VINTAGE: PRICE:

PRODUCER:

REGION & COUNTRY:

GRAPE VARIETY:

RECOMMENDED BY:

PLACE & DATE BOUGHT:

PLACE & DATE TASTED:

APPEARANCE:

NOSE:

TASTE:

FINISH:

OVERALL IMPRESSION:

OVERALL RATINGS: 70 71 72 73 74 75 76 77 78 79
80 81 82 83 84 85 86 87 88 89 90 91 92 93
94 95 96 97 98 99 100

OVERALL VALUE: ★   ★★   ★★★   ★★★★   ★★★★★

TASTING NOTES

WINE:

VINTAGE: PRICE:

PRODUCER:

REGION & COUNTRY:

GRAPE VARIETY:

RECOMMENDED BY:

PLACE & DATE BOUGHT:

PLACE & DATE TASTED:

APPEARANCE:

NOSE:

TASTE:

FINISH:

OVERALL IMPRESSION:

OVERALL RATINGS: 70 71 72 73 74 75 76 77 78 79
80 81 82 83 84 85 86 87 88 89 90 91 92 93
94 95 96 97 98 99 100

OVERALL VALUE: ★   ★★   ★★★   ★★★★   ★★★★★

TASTING NOTES

WINE:

VINTAGE: PRICE:

PRODUCER:

REGION & COUNTRY:

GRAPE VARIETY:

RECOMMENDED BY:

PLACE & DATE BOUGHT:

PLACE & DATE TASTED:

APPEARANCE:

NOSE:

TASTE:

FINISH:

OVERALL IMPRESSION:

OVERALL RATINGS: 70 71 72 73 74 75 76 77 78 79
80 81 82 83 84 85 86 87 88 89 90 91 92 93
94 95 96 97 98 99 100

OVERALL VALUE: ★   ★★   ★★★   ★★★★   ★★★★★

TASTING NOTES

WINE:

VINTAGE: PRICE:

PRODUCER:

REGION & COUNTRY:

GRAPE VARIETY:

RECOMMENDED BY:

PLACE & DATE BOUGHT:

PLACE & DATE TASTED:

APPEARANCE:

NOSE:

TASTE:

FINISH:

OVERALL IMPRESSION:

OVERALL RATINGS: 70 71 72 73 74 75 76 77 78 79
80 81 82 83 84 85 86 87 88 89 90 91 92 93
94 95 96 97 98 99 100

OVERALL VALUE: ★   ★★   ★★★   ★★★★   ★★★★★

TASTING NOTES

WINE:

VINTAGE: PRICE:

PRODUCER:

REGION & COUNTRY:

GRAPE VARIETY:

RECOMMENDED BY:

PLACE & DATE BOUGHT:

PLACE & DATE TASTED:

APPEARANCE:

NOSE:

TASTE:

FINISH:

OVERALL IMPRESSION:

OVERALL RATINGS: 70 71 72 73 74 75 76 77 78 79
80 81 82 83 84 85 86 87 88 89 90 91 92 93
94 95 96 97 98 99 100

OVERALL VALUE: ★   ★★   ★★★   ★★★★   ★★★★★

TASTING NOTES

WINE:

VINTAGE: PRICE:

PRODUCER:

REGION & COUNTRY:

GRAPE VARIETY:

RECOMMENDED BY:

PLACE & DATE BOUGHT:

PLACE & DATE TASTED:

APPEARANCE:

NOSE:

TASTE:

FINISH:

OVERALL IMPRESSION:

OVERALL RATINGS: 70 71 72 73 74 75 76 77 78 79
80 81 82 83 84 85 86 87 88 89 90 91 92 93
94 95 96 97 98 99 100

OVERALL VALUE: ★   ★★   ★★★   ★★★★   ★★★★★

TASTING NOTES

WINE:

VINTAGE: PRICE:

PRODUCER:

REGION & COUNTRY:

GRAPE VARIETY:

RECOMMENDED BY:

PLACE & DATE BOUGHT:

PLACE & DATE TASTED:

APPEARANCE:

NOSE:

TASTE:

FINISH:

OVERALL IMPRESSION:

OVERALL RATINGS: 70 71 72 73 74 75 76 77 78 79
80 81 82 83 84 85 86 87 88 89 90 91 92 93
94 95 96 97 98 99 100

OVERALL VALUE: ★   ★★   ★★★   ★★★★   ★★★★★

TASTING NOTES

WINE:

VINTAGE: PRICE:

PRODUCER:

REGION & COUNTRY:

GRAPE VARIETY:

RECOMMENDED BY:

PLACE & DATE BOUGHT:

PLACE & DATE TASTED:

APPEARANCE:

NOSE:

TASTE:

FINISH:

OVERALL IMPRESSION:

OVERALL RATINGS: 70 71 72 73 74 75 76 77 78 79
80 81 82 83 84 85 86 87 88 89 90 91 92 93
94 95 96 97 98 99 100

OVERALL VALUE: ★   ★★   ★★★   ★★★★   ★★★★★

TASTING NOTES

WINE:

VINTAGE: PRICE:

PRODUCER:

REGION & COUNTRY:

GRAPE VARIETY:

RECOMMENDED BY:

PLACE & DATE BOUGHT:

PLACE & DATE TASTED:

APPEARANCE:

NOSE:

TASTE:

FINISH:

OVERALL IMPRESSION:

OVERALL RATINGS: 70 71 72 73 74 75 76 77 78 79
80 81 82 83 84 85 86 87 88 89 90 91 92 93
94 95 96 97 98 99 100

OVERALL VALUE: ★   ★★   ★★★   ★★★★   ★★★★★

TASTING NOTES

WINE:

VINTAGE: PRICE:

PRODUCER:

REGION & COUNTRY:

GRAPE VARIETY:

RECOMMENDED BY:

PLACE & DATE BOUGHT:

PLACE & DATE TASTED:

APPEARANCE:

NOSE:

TASTE:

FINISH:

OVERALL IMPRESSION:

OVERALL RATINGS: 70 71 72 73 74 75 76 77 78 79
80 81 82 83 84 85 86 87 88 89 90 91 92 93
94 95 96 97 98 99 100

OVERALL VALUE: ★   ★★   ★★★   ★★★★   ★★★★★

TASTING NOTES

WINE:

VINTAGE: PRICE:

PRODUCER:

REGION & COUNTRY:

GRAPE VARIETY:

RECOMMENDED BY:

PLACE & DATE BOUGHT:

PLACE & DATE TASTED:

APPEARANCE:

NOSE:

TASTE:

FINISH:

OVERALL IMPRESSION:

OVERALL RATINGS: 70 71 72 73 74 75 76 77 78 79
80 81 82 83 84 85 86 87 88 89 90 91 92 93
94 95 96 97 98 99 100

OVERALL VALUE: ★   ★★   ★★★   ★★★★   ★★★★★

TASTING NOTES

WINE:

VINTAGE: PRICE:

PRODUCER:

REGION & COUNTRY:

GRAPE VARIETY:

RECOMMENDED BY:

PLACE & DATE BOUGHT:

PLACE & DATE TASTED:

APPEARANCE:

NOSE:

TASTE:

FINISH:

OVERALL IMPRESSION:

OVERALL RATINGS: 70 71 72 73 74 75 76 77 78 79
80 81 82 83 84 85 86 87 88 89 90 91 92 93
94 95 96 97 98 99 100

OVERALL VALUE: ★   ★★   ★★★   ★★★★   ★★★★★

TASTING NOTES

WINE:

VINTAGE: PRICE:

PRODUCER:

REGION & COUNTRY:

GRAPE VARIETY:

RECOMMENDED BY:

PLACE & DATE BOUGHT:

PLACE & DATE TASTED:

APPEARANCE:

NOSE:

TASTE:

FINISH:

OVERALL IMPRESSION:

OVERALL RATINGS: 70 71 72 73 74 75 76 77 78 79

80 81 82 83 84 85 86 87 88 89 90 91 92 93

94 95 96 97 98 99 100

OVERALL VALUE: ★   ★★   ★★★   ★★★★   ★★★★★

TASTING NOTES

WINE:

VINTAGE: PRICE:

PRODUCER:

REGION & COUNTRY:

GRAPE VARIETY:

RECOMMENDED BY:

PLACE & DATE BOUGHT:

PLACE & DATE TASTED:

APPEARANCE:

NOSE:

TASTE:

FINISH:

OVERALL IMPRESSION:

OVERALL RATINGS: 70 71 72 73 74 75 76 77 78 79
80 81 82 83 84 85 86 87 88 89 90 91 92 93
94 95 96 97 98 99 100

OVERALL VALUE: ★   ★★   ★★★   ★★★★   ★★★★★

TASTING NOTES

WINE:

VINTAGE: PRICE:

PRODUCER:

REGION & COUNTRY:

GRAPE VARIETY:

RECOMMENDED BY:

PLACE & DATE BOUGHT:

PLACE & DATE TASTED:

APPEARANCE:

NOSE:

TASTE:

FINISH:

OVERALL IMPRESSION:

OVERALL RATINGS: 70 71 72 73 74 75 76 77 78 79
80 81 82 83 84 85 86 87 88 89 90 91 92 93
94 95 96 97 98 99 100

OVERALL VALUE: ★   ★★   ★★★   ★★★★   ★★★★★

TASTING NOTES

WINE:

VINTAGE: PRICE:

PRODUCER:

REGION & COUNTRY:

GRAPE VARIETY:

RECOMMENDED BY:

PLACE & DATE BOUGHT:

PLACE & DATE TASTED:

APPEARANCE:

NOSE:

TASTE:

FINISH:

OVERALL IMPRESSION:

OVERALL RATINGS: 70 71 72 73 74 75 76 77 78 79
80 81 82 83 84 85 86 87 88 89 90 91 92 93
94 95 96 97 98 99 100

OVERALL VALUE: ★   ★★   ★★★   ★★★★   ★★★★★

TASTING NOTES

WINE:

VINTAGE: PRICE:

PRODUCER:

REGION & COUNTRY:

GRAPE VARIETY:

RECOMMENDED BY:

PLACE & DATE BOUGHT:

PLACE & DATE TASTED:

APPEARANCE:

NOSE:

TASTE:

FINISH:

OVERALL IMPRESSION:

OVERALL RATINGS: 70 71 72 73 74 75 76 77 78 79
80 81 82 83 84 85 86 87 88 89 90 91 92 93
94 95 96 97 98 99 100

OVERALL VALUE: ★   ★★   ★★★   ★★★★   ★★★★★

Tasting Notes

WINE:

VINTAGE: PRICE:

PRODUCER:

REGION & COUNTRY:

GRAPE VARIETY:

RECOMMENDED BY:

PLACE & DATE BOUGHT:

PLACE & DATE TASTED:

APPEARANCE:

NOSE:

TASTE:

FINISH:

OVERALL IMPRESSION:

OVERALL RATINGS: 70 71 72 73 74 75 76 77 78 79
80 81 82 83 84 85 86 87 88 89 90 91 92 93
94 95 96 97 98 99 100

OVERALL VALUE: ★   ★★   ★★★   ★★★★   ★★★★★

*Wine is earth's
answer to the sun.*

Margaret Fuller

*It has become quite
a common proverb that
in wine there is truth.*

Pliny the Elder, *Natural History*

Tasting Notes

WINE:

VINTAGE: PRICE:

PRODUCER:

REGION & COUNTRY:

GRAPE VARIETY:

RECOMMENDED BY:

PLACE & DATE BOUGHT:

PLACE & DATE TASTED:

APPEARANCE:

NOSE:

TASTE:

FINISH:

OVERALL IMPRESSION:

OVERALL RATINGS: 70 71 72 73 74 75 76 77 78 79
80 81 82 83 84 85 86 87 88 89 90 91 92 93
94 95 96 97 98 99 100

OVERALL VALUE: ★   ★★   ★★★   ★★★★   ★★★★★

TASTING NOTES

WINE:

VINTAGE: PRICE:

PRODUCER:

REGION & COUNTRY:

GRAPE VARIETY:

RECOMMENDED BY:

PLACE & DATE BOUGHT:

PLACE & DATE TASTED:

APPEARANCE:

NOSE:

TASTE:

FINISH:

OVERALL IMPRESSION:

OVERALL RATINGS: 70 71 72 73 74 75 76 77 78 79
80 81 82 83 84 85 86 87 88 89 90 91 92 93
94 95 96 97 98 99 100

OVERALL VALUE: ★   ★★   ★★★   ★★★★   ★★★★★

TASTING NOTES

WINE:

VINTAGE: PRICE:

PRODUCER:

REGION & COUNTRY:

GRAPE VARIETY:

RECOMMENDED BY:

PLACE & DATE BOUGHT:

PLACE & DATE TASTED:

APPEARANCE:

NOSE:

TASTE:

FINISH:

OVERALL IMPRESSION:

OVERALL RATINGS: 70 71 72 73 74 75 76 77 78 79
80 81 82 83 84 85 86 87 88 89 90 91 92 93
94 95 96 97 98 99 100

OVERALL VALUE: ★   ★★   ★★★   ★★★★   ★★★★★

TASTING NOTES

WINE:

VINTAGE: PRICE:

PRODUCER:

REGION & COUNTRY:

GRAPE VARIETY:

RECOMMENDED BY:

PLACE & DATE BOUGHT:

PLACE & DATE TASTED:

APPEARANCE:

NOSE:

TASTE:

FINISH:

OVERALL IMPRESSION:

OVERALL RATINGS: 70 71 72 73 74 75 76 77 78 79
80 81 82 83 84 85 86 87 88 89 90 91 92 93
94 95 96 97 98 99 100

OVERALL VALUE: ★   ★★   ★★★   ★★★★   ★★★★★

TASTING NOTES

WINE:

VINTAGE: PRICE:

PRODUCER:

REGION & COUNTRY:

GRAPE VARIETY:

RECOMMENDED BY:

PLACE & DATE BOUGHT:

PLACE & DATE TASTED:

APPEARANCE:

NOSE:

TASTE:

FINISH:

OVERALL IMPRESSION:

OVERALL RATINGS: 70 71 72 73 74 75 76 77 78 79
80 81 82 83 84 85 86 87 88 89 90 91 92 93
94 95 96 97 98 99 100

OVERALL VALUE: ★   ★★   ★★★   ★★★★   ★★★★★

TASTING NOTES

WINE:

VINTAGE: PRICE:

PRODUCER:

REGION & COUNTRY:

GRAPE VARIETY:

RECOMMENDED BY:

PLACE & DATE BOUGHT:

PLACE & DATE TASTED:

APPEARANCE:

NOSE:

TASTE:

FINISH:

OVERALL IMPRESSION:

OVERALL RATINGS: 70 71 72 73 74 75 76 77 78 79
80 81 82 83 84 85 86 87 88 89 90 91 92 93
94 95 96 97 98 99 100

OVERALL VALUE: ★   ★★   ★★★   ★★★★   ★★★★★

TASTING NOTES

WINE:

VINTAGE: PRICE:

PRODUCER:

REGION & COUNTRY:

GRAPE VARIETY:

RECOMMENDED BY:

PLACE & DATE BOUGHT:

PLACE & DATE TASTED:

APPEARANCE:

NOSE:

TASTE:

FINISH:

OVERALL IMPRESSION:

OVERALL RATINGS: 70 71 72 73 74 75 76 77 78 79
80 81 82 83 84 85 86 87 88 89 90 91 92 93
94 95 96 97 98 99 100

OVERALL VALUE: ★   ★★   ★★★   ★★★★   ★★★★★

TASTING NOTES

WINE:

VINTAGE: PRICE:

PRODUCER:

REGION & COUNTRY:

GRAPE VARIETY:

RECOMMENDED BY:

PLACE & DATE BOUGHT:

PLACE & DATE TASTED:

APPEARANCE:

NOSE:

TASTE:

FINISH:

OVERALL IMPRESSION:

OVERALL RATINGS: 70 71 72 73 74 75 76 77 78 79
80 81 82 83 84 85 86 87 88 89 90 91 92 93
94 95 96 97 98 99 100

OVERALL VALUE: ★   ★★   ★★★   ★★★★   ★★★★★

TASTING NOTES

WINE:

VINTAGE: PRICE:

PRODUCER:

REGION & COUNTRY:

GRAPE VARIETY:

RECOMMENDED BY:

PLACE & DATE BOUGHT:

PLACE & DATE TASTED:

APPEARANCE:

NOSE:

TASTE:

FINISH:

OVERALL IMPRESSION:

OVERALL RATINGS: 70 71 72 73 74 75 76 77 78 79
80 81 82 83 84 85 86 87 88 89 90 91 92 93
94 95 96 97 98 99 100

OVERALL VALUE: ★   ★★   ★★★   ★★★★   ★★★★★

TASTING NOTES

WINE:

VINTAGE: PRICE:

PRODUCER:

REGION & COUNTRY:

GRAPE VARIETY:

RECOMMENDED BY:

PLACE & DATE BOUGHT:

PLACE & DATE TASTED:

APPEARANCE:

NOSE:

TASTE:

FINISH:

OVERALL IMPRESSION:

OVERALL RATINGS: 70 71 72 73 74 75 76 77 78 79
80 81 82 83 84 85 86 87 88 89 90 91 92 93
94 95 96 97 98 99 100

OVERALL VALUE: ★   ★★   ★★★   ★★★★   ★★★★★

TASTING NOTES

WINE:

VINTAGE: PRICE:

PRODUCER:

REGION & COUNTRY:

GRAPE VARIETY:

RECOMMENDED BY:

PLACE & DATE BOUGHT:

PLACE & DATE TASTED:

APPEARANCE:

NOSE:

TASTE:

FINISH:

OVERALL IMPRESSION:

OVERALL RATINGS: 70   71   72   73   74   75   76   77   78   79
80   81   82   83   84   85   86   87   88   89   90   91   92   93
94   95   96   97   98   99   100

OVERALL VALUE: ★   ★★   ★★★   ★★★★   ★★★★★

Tasting Notes

WINE:

VINTAGE: PRICE:

PRODUCER:

REGION & COUNTRY:

GRAPE VARIETY:

RECOMMENDED BY:

PLACE & DATE BOUGHT:

PLACE & DATE TASTED:

APPEARANCE:

NOSE:

TASTE:

FINISH:

OVERALL IMPRESSION:

OVERALL RATINGS: 70 71 72 73 74 75 76 77 78 79
80 81 82 83 84 85 86 87 88 89 90 91 92 93
94 95 96 97 98 99 100

OVERALL VALUE: ★   ★★   ★★★   ★★★★   ★★★★★

TASTING NOTES

WINE:

VINTAGE: PRICE:

PRODUCER:

REGION & COUNTRY:

GRAPE VARIETY:

RECOMMENDED BY:

PLACE & DATE BOUGHT:

PLACE & DATE TASTED:

APPEARANCE:

NOSE:

TASTE:

FINISH:

OVERALL IMPRESSION:

OVERALL RATINGS: 70 71 72 73 74 75 76 77 78 79
80 81 82 83 84 85 86 87 88 89 90 91 92 93
94 95 96 97 98 99 100

OVERALL VALUE: ★   ★★   ★★★   ★★★★   ★★★★★

TASTING NOTES

WINE:

VINTAGE: PRICE:

PRODUCER:

REGION & COUNTRY:

GRAPE VARIETY:

RECOMMENDED BY:

PLACE & DATE BOUGHT:

PLACE & DATE TASTED:

APPEARANCE:

NOSE:

TASTE:

FINISH:

OVERALL IMPRESSION:

OVERALL RATINGS: 70 71 72 73 74 75 76 77 78 79
80 81 82 83 84 85 86 87 88 89 90 91 92 93
94 95 96 97 98 99 100

OVERALL VALUE: ★   ★★   ★★★   ★★★★   ★★★★★

TASTING NOTES

WINE:

VINTAGE: PRICE:

PRODUCER:

REGION & COUNTRY:

GRAPE VARIETY:

RECOMMENDED BY:

PLACE & DATE BOUGHT:

PLACE & DATE TASTED:

APPEARANCE:

NOSE:

TASTE:

FINISH:

OVERALL IMPRESSION:

OVERALL RATINGS: 70   71   72   73   74   75   76   77   78   79
80   81   82   83   84   85   86   87   88   89   90   91   92   93
94   95   96   97   98   99   100

OVERALL VALUE: ★   ★★   ★★★   ★★★★   ★★★★★

TASTING NOTES

WINE:

VINTAGE: PRICE:

PRODUCER:

REGION & COUNTRY:

GRAPE VARIETY:

RECOMMENDED BY:

PLACE & DATE BOUGHT:

PLACE & DATE TASTED:

APPEARANCE:

NOSE:

TASTE:

FINISH:

OVERALL IMPRESSION:

OVERALL RATINGS: 70 71 72 73 74 75 76 77 78 79
80 81 82 83 84 85 86 87 88 89 90 91 92 93
94 95 96 97 98 99 100

OVERALL VALUE: ★   ★★   ★★★   ★★★★   ★★★★★

TASTING NOTES

WINE:

VINTAGE: PRICE:

PRODUCER:

REGION & COUNTRY:

GRAPE VARIETY:

RECOMMENDED BY:

PLACE & DATE BOUGHT:

PLACE & DATE TASTED:

APPEARANCE:

NOSE:

TASTE:

FINISH:

OVERALL IMPRESSION:

OVERALL RATINGS: 70 71 72 73 74 75 76 77 78 79
80 81 82 83 84 85 86 87 88 89 90 91 92 93
94 95 96 97 98 99 100

OVERALL VALUE: ★   ★★   ★★★   ★★★★   ★★★★★

TASTING NOTES

WINE:

VINTAGE: PRICE:

PRODUCER:

REGION & COUNTRY:

GRAPE VARIETY:

RECOMMENDED BY:

PLACE & DATE BOUGHT:

PLACE & DATE TASTED:

APPEARANCE:

NOSE:

TASTE:

FINISH:

OVERALL IMPRESSION:

OVERALL RATINGS: 70 71 72 73 74 75 76 77 78 79
80 81 82 83 84 85 86 87 88 89 90 91 92 93
94 95 96 97 98 99 100

OVERALL VALUE: ★   ★★   ★★★   ★★★★   ★★★★★

TASTING NOTES

WINE:

VINTAGE: PRICE:

PRODUCER:

REGION & COUNTRY:

GRAPE VARIETY:

RECOMMENDED BY:

PLACE & DATE BOUGHT:

PLACE & DATE TASTED:

APPEARANCE:

NOSE:

TASTE:

FINISH:

OVERALL IMPRESSION:

OVERALL RATINGS: 70 71 72 73 74 75 76 77 78 79
80 81 82 83 84 85 86 87 88 89 90 91 92 93
94 95 96 97 98 99 100

OVERALL VALUE: ★   ★★   ★★★   ★★★★   ★★★★★

TASTING NOTES

WINE:

VINTAGE: PRICE:

PRODUCER:

REGION & COUNTRY:

GRAPE VARIETY:

RECOMMENDED BY:

PLACE & DATE BOUGHT:

PLACE & DATE TASTED:

APPEARANCE:

NOSE:

TASTE:

FINISH:

OVERALL IMPRESSION:

OVERALL RATINGS: 70 71 72 73 74 75 76 77 78 79
80 81 82 83 84 85 86 87 88 89 90 91 92 93
94 95 96 97 98 99 100

OVERALL VALUE: ★   ★★   ★★★   ★★★★   ★★★★★

TASTING NOTES

WINE:

VINTAGE: PRICE:

PRODUCER:

REGION & COUNTRY:

GRAPE VARIETY:

RECOMMENDED BY:

PLACE & DATE BOUGHT:

PLACE & DATE TASTED:

APPEARANCE:

NOSE:

TASTE:

FINISH:

OVERALL IMPRESSION:

OVERALL RATINGS: 70 71 72 73 74 75 76 77 78 79
80 81 82 83 84 85 86 87 88 89 90 91 92 93
94 95 96 97 98 99 100

OVERALL VALUE: ★   ★★   ★★★   ★★★★   ★★★★★

TASTING NOTES

WINE:

VINTAGE: PRICE:

PRODUCER:

REGION & COUNTRY:

GRAPE VARIETY:

RECOMMENDED BY:

PLACE & DATE BOUGHT:

PLACE & DATE TASTED:

APPEARANCE:

NOSE:

TASTE:

FINISH:

OVERALL IMPRESSION:

OVERALL RATINGS: 70 71 72 73 74 75 76 77 78 79
80 81 82 83 84 85 86 87 88 89 90 91 92 93
94 95 96 97 98 99 100

OVERALL VALUE: ★   ★★   ★★★   ★★★★   ★★★★★

TASTING NOTES

WINE:

VINTAGE: PRICE:

PRODUCER:

REGION & COUNTRY:

GRAPE VARIETY:

RECOMMENDED BY:

PLACE & DATE BOUGHT:

PLACE & DATE TASTED:

APPEARANCE:

NOSE:

TASTE:

FINISH:

OVERALL IMPRESSION:

OVERALL RATINGS: 70 71 72 73 74 75 76 77 78 79
80 81 82 83 84 85 86 87 88 89 90 91 92 93
94 95 96 97 98 99 100

OVERALL VALUE: ★   ★★   ★★★   ★★★★   ★★★★★

TASTING NOTES

WINE:

VINTAGE: PRICE:

PRODUCER:

REGION & COUNTRY:

GRAPE VARIETY:

RECOMMENDED BY:

PLACE & DATE BOUGHT:

PLACE & DATE TASTED:

APPEARANCE:

NOSE:

TASTE:

FINISH:

OVERALL IMPRESSION:

OVERALL RATINGS: 70 71 72 73 74 75 76 77 78 79
80 81 82 83 84 85 86 87 88 89 90 91 92 93
94 95 96 97 98 99 100

OVERALL VALUE: ★   ★★   ★★★   ★★★★   ★★★★★

TASTING NOTES

WINE:

VINTAGE: PRICE:

PRODUCER:

REGION & COUNTRY:

GRAPE VARIETY:

RECOMMENDED BY:

PLACE & DATE BOUGHT:

PLACE & DATE TASTED:

APPEARANCE:

NOSE:

TASTE:

FINISH:

OVERALL IMPRESSION:

OVERALL RATINGS: 70 71 72 73 74 75 76 77 78 79
80 81 82 83 84 85 86 87 88 89 90 91 92 93
94 95 96 97 98 99 100

OVERALL VALUE: ★   ★★   ★★★   ★★★★   ★★★★★

TASTING NOTES

WINE:

VINTAGE: PRICE:

PRODUCER:

REGION & COUNTRY:

GRAPE VARIETY:

RECOMMENDED BY:

PLACE & DATE BOUGHT:

PLACE & DATE TASTED:

APPEARANCE:

NOSE:

TASTE:

FINISH:

OVERALL IMPRESSION:

OVERALL RATINGS: 70 71 72 73 74 75 76 77 78 79
80 81 82 83 84 85 86 87 88 89 90 91 92 93
94 95 96 97 98 99 100

OVERALL VALUE: ★   ★★   ★★★   ★★★★   ★★★★★

TASTING NOTES

WINE:

VINTAGE: PRICE:

PRODUCER:

REGION & COUNTRY:

GRAPE VARIETY:

RECOMMENDED BY:

PLACE & DATE BOUGHT:

PLACE & DATE TASTED:

APPEARANCE:

NOSE:

TASTE:

FINISH:

OVERALL IMPRESSION:

OVERALL RATINGS: 70 71 72 73 74 75 76 77 78 79
80 81 82 83 84 85 86 87 88 89 90 91 92 93
94 95 96 97 98 99 100

OVERALL VALUE: ★   ★★   ★★★   ★★★★   ★★★★★

TASTING NOTES

WINE:

VINTAGE: PRICE:

PRODUCER:

REGION & COUNTRY:

GRAPE VARIETY:

RECOMMENDED BY:

PLACE & DATE BOUGHT:

PLACE & DATE TASTED:

APPEARANCE:

NOSE:

TASTE:

FINISH:

OVERALL IMPRESSION:

OVERALL RATINGS: 70 71 72 73 74 75 76 77 78 79
80 81 82 83 84 85 86 87 88 89 90 91 92 93
94 95 96 97 98 99 100

OVERALL VALUE: ★   ★★   ★★★   ★★★★   ★★★★★

TASTING NOTES

WINE:

VINTAGE: PRICE:

PRODUCER:

REGION & COUNTRY:

GRAPE VARIETY:

RECOMMENDED BY:

PLACE & DATE BOUGHT:

PLACE & DATE TASTED:

APPEARANCE:

NOSE:

TASTE:

FINISH:

OVERALL IMPRESSION:

OVERALL RATINGS: 70 71 72 73 74 75 76 77 78 79
80 81 82 83 84 85 86 87 88 89 90 91 92 93
94 95 96 97 98 99 100

OVERALL VALUE: ★   ★★   ★★★   ★★★★   ★★★★★

*One barrel of wine
can work more miracles
than a church full
of saints.*

Italian proverb

❖

*Nothing more excellent
or valuable than
wine was ever granted
by the Gods to man.*

Plato

TASTING NOTES

WINE:

VINTAGE: PRICE:

PRODUCER:

REGION & COUNTRY:

GRAPE VARIETY:

RECOMMENDED BY:

PLACE & DATE BOUGHT:

PLACE & DATE TASTED:

APPEARANCE:

NOSE:

TASTE:

FINISH:

OVERALL IMPRESSION:

OVERALL RATINGS: 70   71   72   73   74   75   76   77   78   79
80   81   82   83   84   85   86   87   88   89   90   91   92   93
94   95   96   97   98   99   100

OVERALL VALUE: ★   ★★   ★★★   ★★★★   ★★★★★

TASTING NOTES

WINE:

VINTAGE: PRICE:

PRODUCER:

REGION & COUNTRY:

GRAPE VARIETY:

RECOMMENDED BY:

PLACE & DATE BOUGHT:

PLACE & DATE TASTED:

APPEARANCE:

NOSE:

TASTE:

FINISH:

OVERALL IMPRESSION:

OVERALL RATINGS: 70 71 72 73 74 75 76 77 78 79
80 81 82 83 84 85 86 87 88 89 90 91 92 93
94 95 96 97 98 99 100

OVERALL VALUE: ★   ★★   ★★★   ★★★★   ★★★★★

TASTING NOTES

WINE:

VINTAGE: PRICE:

PRODUCER:

REGION & COUNTRY:

GRAPE VARIETY:

RECOMMENDED BY:

PLACE & DATE BOUGHT:

PLACE & DATE TASTED:

APPEARANCE:

NOSE:

TASTE:

FINISH:

OVERALL IMPRESSION:

OVERALL RATINGS: 70 71 72 73 74 75 76 77 78 79
80 81 82 83 84 85 86 87 88 89 90 91 92 93
94 95 96 97 98 99 100

OVERALL VALUE: ★   ★★   ★★★   ★★★★   ★★★★★

TASTING NOTES

WINE:

VINTAGE: PRICE:

PRODUCER:

REGION & COUNTRY:

GRAPE VARIETY:

RECOMMENDED BY:

PLACE & DATE BOUGHT:

PLACE & DATE TASTED:

APPEARANCE:

NOSE:

TASTE:

FINISH:

OVERALL IMPRESSION:

OVERALL RATINGS: 70 71 72 73 74 75 76 77 78 79
80 81 82 83 84 85 86 87 88 89 90 91 92 93
94 95 96 97 98 99 100

OVERALL VALUE: ★   ★★   ★★★   ★★★★   ★★★★★

TASTING NOTES

WINE:

VINTAGE: PRICE:

PRODUCER:

REGION & COUNTRY:

GRAPE VARIETY:

RECOMMENDED BY:

PLACE & DATE BOUGHT:

PLACE & DATE TASTED:

APPEARANCE:

NOSE:

TASTE:

FINISH:

OVERALL IMPRESSION:

OVERALL RATINGS: 70 71 72 73 74 75 76 77 78 79
80 81 82 83 84 85 86 87 88 89 90 91 92 93
94 95 96 97 98 99 100

OVERALL VALUE: ★   ★★   ★★★   ★★★★   ★★★★★

TASTING NOTES

WINE:

VINTAGE: PRICE:

PRODUCER:

REGION & COUNTRY:

GRAPE VARIETY:

RECOMMENDED BY:

PLACE & DATE BOUGHT:

PLACE & DATE TASTED:

APPEARANCE:

NOSE:

TASTE:

FINISH:

OVERALL IMPRESSION:

OVERALL RATINGS: 70   71   72   73   74   75   76   77   78   79
80   81   82   83   84   85   86   87   88   89   90   91   92   93
94   95   96   97   98   99   100

OVERALL VALUE: ★   ★★   ★★★   ★★★★   ★★★★★

TASTING NOTES

WINE:

VINTAGE: PRICE:

PRODUCER:

REGION & COUNTRY:

GRAPE VARIETY:

RECOMMENDED BY:

PLACE & DATE BOUGHT:

PLACE & DATE TASTED:

APPEARANCE:

NOSE:

TASTE:

FINISH:

OVERALL IMPRESSION:

OVERALL RATINGS: 70 71 72 73 74 75 76 77 78 79
80 81 82 83 84 85 86 87 88 89 90 91 92 93
94 95 96 97 98 99 100

OVERALL VALUE: ★ ★★ ★★★ ★★★★ ★★★★★

TASTING NOTES

WINE:

VINTAGE: PRICE:

PRODUCER:

REGION & COUNTRY:

GRAPE VARIETY:

RECOMMENDED BY:

PLACE & DATE BOUGHT:

PLACE & DATE TASTED:

APPEARANCE:

NOSE:

TASTE:

FINISH:

OVERALL IMPRESSION:

OVERALL RATINGS: 70 71 72 73 74 75 76 77 78 79
80 81 82 83 84 85 86 87 88 89 90 91 92 93
94 95 96 97 98 99 100

OVERALL VALUE: ★   ★★   ★★★   ★★★★   ★★★★★

TASTING NOTES

WINE:

VINTAGE: PRICE:

PRODUCER:

REGION & COUNTRY:

GRAPE VARIETY:

RECOMMENDED BY:

PLACE & DATE BOUGHT:

PLACE & DATE TASTED:

APPEARANCE:

NOSE:

TASTE:

FINISH:

OVERALL IMPRESSION:

OVERALL RATINGS: 70 71 72 73 74 75 76 77 78 79
80 81 82 83 84 85 86 87 88 89 90 91 92 93
94 95 96 97 98 99 100

OVERALL VALUE: ★   ★★   ★★★   ★★★★   ★★★★★

TASTING NOTES

WINE:

VINTAGE: PRICE:

PRODUCER:

REGION & COUNTRY:

GRAPE VARIETY:

RECOMMENDED BY:

PLACE & DATE BOUGHT:

PLACE & DATE TASTED:

APPEARANCE:

NOSE:

TASTE:

FINISH:

OVERALL IMPRESSION:

OVERALL RATINGS: 70 71 72 73 74 75 76 77 78 79
80 81 82 83 84 85 86 87 88 89 90 91 92 93
94 95 96 97 98 99 100

OVERALL VALUE: ★   ★★   ★★★   ★★★★   ★★★★★

TASTING NOTES

WINE:

VINTAGE: PRICE:

PRODUCER:

REGION & COUNTRY:

GRAPE VARIETY:

RECOMMENDED BY:

PLACE & DATE BOUGHT:

PLACE & DATE TASTED:

APPEARANCE:

NOSE:

TASTE:

FINISH:

OVERALL IMPRESSION:

OVERALL RATINGS: 70 71 72 73 74 75 76 77 78 79
80 81 82 83 84 85 86 87 88 89 90 91 92 93
94 95 96 97 98 99 100

OVERALL VALUE: ★   ★★   ★★★   ★★★★   ★★★★★

TASTING NOTES

WINE:

VINTAGE: PRICE:

PRODUCER:

REGION & COUNTRY:

GRAPE VARIETY:

RECOMMENDED BY:

PLACE & DATE BOUGHT:

PLACE & DATE TASTED:

APPEARANCE:

NOSE:

TASTE:

FINISH:

OVERALL IMPRESSION.

OVERALL RATINGS: 70 71 72 73 74 75 76 77 78 79
80 81 82 83 84 85 86 87 88 89 90 91 92 93
94 95 96 97 98 99 100

OVERALL VALUE: ★   ★★   ★★★   ★★★★   ★★★★★

Tasting Notes

WINE:

VINTAGE: PRICE:

PRODUCER:

REGION & COUNTRY:

GRAPE VARIETY:

RECOMMENDED BY:

PLACE & DATE BOUGHT:

PLACE & DATE TASTED:

APPEARANCE:

NOSE:

TASTE:

FINISH:

OVERALL IMPRESSION:

OVERALL RATINGS: 70 71 72 73 74 75 76 77 78 79
80 81 82 83 84 85 86 87 88 89 90 91 92 93
94 95 96 97 98 99 100

OVERALL VALUE: ★   ★★   ★★★   ★★★★   ★★★★★

TASTING NOTES

WINE:

VINTAGE: PRICE:

PRODUCER:

REGION & COUNTRY:

GRAPE VARIETY:

RECOMMENDED BY:

PLACE & DATE BOUGHT:

PLACE & DATE TASTED:

APPEARANCE:

NOSE:

TASTE:

FINISH:

OVERALL IMPRESSION:

OVERALL RATINGS: 70 71 72 73 74 75 76 77 78 79
80 81 82 83 84 85 86 87 88 89 90 91 92 93
94 95 96 97 98 99 100

OVERALL VALUE: ★   ★★   ★★★   ★★★★   ★★★★★

TASTING NOTES

WINE:

VINTAGE: PRICE:

PRODUCER:

REGION & COUNTRY:

GRAPE VARIETY:

RECOMMENDED BY:

PLACE & DATE BOUGHT:

PLACE & DATE TASTED:

APPEARANCE:

NOSE:

TASTE:

FINISH:

OVERALL IMPRESSION:

OVERALL RATINGS: 70 71 72 73 74 75 76 77 78 79
80 81 82 83 84 85 86 87 88 89 90 91 92 93
94 95 96 97 98 99 100

OVERALL VALUE: ★   ★★   ★★★   ★★★★   ★★★★★

TASTING NOTES

WINE:

VINTAGE: PRICE:

PRODUCER:

REGION & COUNTRY:

GRAPE VARIETY:

RECOMMENDED BY:

PLACE & DATE BOUGHT:

PLACE & DATE TASTED:

APPEARANCE:

NOSE:

TASTE:

FINISH:

OVERALL IMPRESSION:

OVERALL RATINGS: 70 71 72 73 74 75 76 77 78 79
80 81 82 83 84 85 86 87 88 89 90 91 92 93
94 95 96 97 98 99 100

OVERALL VALUE: ★   ★★   ★★★   ★★★★   ★★★★★

TASTING NOTES

WINE:

VINTAGE: PRICE:

PRODUCER:

REGION & COUNTRY:

GRAPE VARIETY:

RECOMMENDED BY:

PLACE & DATE BOUGHT:

PLACE & DATE TASTED:

APPEARANCE:

NOSE:

TASTE:

FINISH:

OVERALL IMPRESSION:

OVERALL RATINGS: 70 71 72 73 74 75 76 77 78 79
80 81 82 83 84 85 86 87 88 89 90 91 92 93
94 95 96 97 98 99 100

OVERALL VALUE: ★   ★★   ★★★   ★★★★   ★★★★★

TASTING NOTES

WINE:

VINTAGE: PRICE:

PRODUCER:

REGION & COUNTRY:

GRAPE VARIETY:

RECOMMENDED BY:

PLACE & DATE BOUGHT:

PLACE & DATE TASTED:

APPEARANCE:

NOSE:

TASTE:

FINISH:

OVERALL IMPRESSION:

OVERALL RATINGS: 70 71 72 73 74 75 76 77 78 79
80 81 82 83 84 85 86 87 88 89 90 91 92 93
94 95 96 97 98 99 100

OVERALL VALUE: ★   ★★   ★★★   ★★★★   ★★★★★

TASTING NOTES

WINE:

VINTAGE: PRICE:

PRODUCER:

REGION & COUNTRY:

GRAPE VARIETY:

RECOMMENDED BY:

PLACE & DATE BOUGHT:

PLACE & DATE TASTED:

APPEARANCE:

NOSE:

TASTE:

FINISH:

OVERALL IMPRESSION:

OVERALL RATINGS: 70 71 72 73 74 75 76 77 78 79
80 81 82 83 84 85 86 87 88 89 90 91 92 93
94 95 96 97 98 99 100

OVERALL VALUE: ★   ★★   ★★★   ★★★★   ★★★★★

TASTING NOTES

WINE:

VINTAGE: PRICE:

PRODUCER:

REGION & COUNTRY:

GRAPE VARIETY:

RECOMMENDED BY:

PLACE & DATE BOUGHT:

PLACE & DATE TASTED:

APPEARANCE:

NOSE:

TASTE:

FINISH:

OVERALL IMPRESSION:

OVERALL RATINGS: 70 71 72 73 74 75 76 77 78 79
80 81 82 83 84 85 86 87 88 89 90 91 92 93
94 95 96 97 98 99 100

OVERALL VALUE: ★   ★★   ★★★   ★★★★   ★★★★★

TASTING NOTES

WINE:

VINTAGE: PRICE:

PRODUCER:

REGION & COUNTRY:

GRAPE VARIETY:

RECOMMENDED BY:

PLACE & DATE BOUGHT:

PLACE & DATE TASTED:

APPEARANCE:

NOSE:

TASTE:

FINISH:

OVERALL IMPRESSION:

OVERALL RATINGS: 70 71 72 73 74 75 76 77 78 79
80 81 82 83 84 85 86 87 88 89 90 91 92 93
94 95 96 97 98 99 100

OVERALL VALUE: ★   ★★   ★★★   ★★★★   ★★★★★

TASTING NOTES

WINE:

VINTAGE: PRICE:

PRODUCER:

REGION & COUNTRY:

GRAPE VARIETY:

RECOMMENDED BY:

PLACE & DATE BOUGHT:

PLACE & DATE TASTED:

APPEARANCE:

NOSE:

TASTE:

FINISH:

OVERALL IMPRESSION:

OVERALL RATINGS: 70 71 72 73 74 75 76 77 78 79
80 81 82 83 84 85 86 87 88 89 90 91 92 93
94 95 96 97 98 99 100

OVERALL VALUE: ★   ★★   ★★★   ★★★★   ★★★★★

TASTING NOTES

WINE:

VINTAGE: PRICE:

PRODUCER:

REGION & COUNTRY:

GRAPE VARIETY:

RECOMMENDED BY:

PLACE & DATE BOUGHT:

PLACE & DATE TASTED:

APPEARANCE:

NOSE:

TASTE:

FINISH:

OVERALL IMPRESSION:

OVERALL RATINGS: 70 71 72 73 74 75 76 77 78 79
80 81 82 83 84 85 86 87 88 89 90 91 92 93
94 95 96 97 98 99 100

OVERALL VALUE: ★   ★★   ★★★   ★★★★   ★★★★★

TASTING NOTES

WINE:

VINTAGE: PRICE:

PRODUCER:

REGION & COUNTRY:

GRAPE VARIETY:

RECOMMENDED BY:

PLACE & DATE BOUGHT:

PLACE & DATE TASTED:

APPEARANCE:

NOSE:

TASTE:

FINISH:

OVERALL IMPRESSION:

OVERALL RATINGS: 70 71 72 73 74 75 76 77 78 79
80 81 82 83 84 85 86 87 88 89 90 91 92 93
94 95 96 97 98 99 100

OVERALL VALUE: ★   ★★   ★★★   ★★★★   ★★★★★

TASTING NOTES

WINE:

VINTAGE: PRICE:

PRODUCER:

REGION & COUNTRY:

GRAPE VARIETY:

RECOMMENDED BY:

PLACE & DATE BOUGHT:

PLACE & DATE TASTED:

APPEARANCE:

NOSE:

TASTE:

FINISH:

OVERALL IMPRESSION:

OVERALL RATINGS: 70 71 72 73 74 75 76 77 78 79
80 81 82 83 84 85 86 87 88 89 90 91 92 93
94 95 96 97 98 99 100

OVERALL VALUE: ★   ★★   ★★★   ★★★★   ★★★★★

TASTING NOTES

WINE:

VINTAGE: PRICE:

PRODUCER:

REGION & COUNTRY:

GRAPE VARIETY:

RECOMMENDED BY:

PLACE & DATE BOUGHT:

PLACE & DATE TASTED:

APPEARANCE:

NOSE:

TASTE:

FINISH:

OVERALL IMPRESSION:

OVERALL RATINGS: 70 71 72 73 74 75 76 77 78 79
80 81 82 83 84 85 86 87 88 89 90 91 92 93
94 95 96 97 98 99 100

OVERALL VALUE: ★   ★★   ★★★   ★★★★   ★★★★★

TASTING NOTES

WINE:

VINTAGE: PRICE:

PRODUCER:

REGION & COUNTRY:

GRAPE VARIETY:

RECOMMENDED BY:

PLACE & DATE BOUGHT:

PLACE & DATE TASTED:

APPEARANCE:

NOSE:

TASTE:

FINISH:

OVERALL IMPRESSION:

OVERALL RATINGS: 70 71 72 73 74 75 76 77 78 79
80 81 82 83 84 85 86 87 88 89 90 91 92 93
94 95 96 97 98 99 100

OVERALL VALUE: ★   ★★   ★★★   ★★★★   ★★★★★

TASTING NOTES

WINE:

VINTAGE: PRICE:

PRODUCER:

REGION & COUNTRY:

GRAPE VARIETY:

RECOMMENDED BY:

PLACE & DATE BOUGHT:

PLACE & DATE TASTED:

APPEARANCE:

NOSE:

TASTE:

FINISH:

OVERALL IMPRESSION:

OVERALL RATINGS: 70 71 72 73 74 75 76 77 78 79
80 81 82 83 84 85 86 87 88 89 90 91 92 93
94 95 96 97 98 99 100

OVERALL VALUE: ★   ★★   ★★★   ★★★★   ★★★★★

TASTING NOTES

WINE:

VINTAGE: PRICE:

PRODUCER:

REGION & COUNTRY:

GRAPE VARIETY:

RECOMMENDED BY:

PLACE & DATE BOUGHT:

PLACE & DATE TASTED:

APPEARANCE:

NOSE:

TASTE:

FINISH:

OVERALL IMPRESSION:

OVERALL RATINGS: 70 71 72 73 74 75 76 77 78 79
80 81 82 83 84 85 86 87 88 89 90 91 92 93
94 95 96 97 98 99 100

OVERALL VALUE: ★   ★★   ★★★   ★★★★   ★★★★★

*Have confidence in
your own palate—it
is, after all, the only
one you will ever
need to impress.*

Joseph DeLissio,
The River Café Wine Primer

❖

TASTING NOTES

WINE:

VINTAGE: PRICE:

PRODUCER:

REGION & COUNTRY:

GRAPE VARIETY:

RECOMMENDED BY:

PLACE & DATE BOUGHT:

PLACE & DATE TASTED:

APPEARANCE:

NOSE:

TASTE:

FINISH:

OVERALL IMPRESSION:

OVERALL RATINGS: 70 71 72 73 74 75 76 77 78 79
80 81 82 83 84 85 86 87 88 89 90 91 92 93
94 95 96 97 98 99 100

OVERALL VALUE: ★   ★★   ★★★   ★★★★   ★★★★★

TASTING NOTES

WINE:

VINTAGE: PRICE:

PRODUCER:

REGION & COUNTRY:

GRAPE VARIETY:

RECOMMENDED BY:

PLACE & DATE BOUGHT:

PLACE & DATE TASTED:

APPEARANCE:

NOSE:

TASTE:

FINISH:

OVERALL IMPRESSION:

OVERALL RATINGS: 70 71 72 73 74 75 76 77 78 79
80 81 82 83 84 85 86 87 88 89 90 91 92 93
94 95 96 97 98 99 100

OVERALL VALUE: ★   ★★   ★★★   ★★★★   ★★★★★

TASTING NOTES

WINE:

VINTAGE: PRICE:

PRODUCER:

REGION & COUNTRY:

GRAPE VARIETY:

RECOMMENDED BY:

PLACE & DATE BOUGHT:

PLACE & DATE TASTED:

APPEARANCE:

NOSE:

TASTE:

FINISH:

OVERALL IMPRESSION:

OVERALL RATINGS: 70 71 72 73 74 75 76 77 78 79
80 81 82 83 84 85 86 87 88 89 90 91 92 93
94 95 96 97 98 99 100

OVERALL VALUE: ★   ★★   ★★★   ★★★★   ★★★★★

TASTING NOTES

WINE:

VINTAGE: PRICE:

PRODUCER:

REGION & COUNTRY:

GRAPE VARIETY:

RECOMMENDED BY:

PLACE & DATE BOUGHT:

PLACE & DATE TASTED:

APPEARANCE:

NOSE:

TASTE:

FINISH:

OVERALL IMPRESSION:

OVERALL RATINGS: 70 71 72 73 74 75 76 77 78 79
80 81 82 83 84 85 86 87 88 89 90 91 92 93
94 95 96 97 98 99 100

OVERALL VALUE: ★   ★★   ★★★   ★★★★   ★★★★★

ASTING NOTES

WINE:

VINTAGE: PRICE:

PRODUCER:

REGION & COUNTRY:

GRAPE VARIETY:

RECOMMENDED BY:

PLACE & DATE BOUGHT:

PLACE & DATE TASTED:

APPEARANCE:

NOSE:

TASTE:

FINISH:

OVERALL IMPRESSION:

OVERALL RATINGS: 70 71 72 73 74 75 76 77 78 79
80 81 82 83 84 85 86 87 88 89 90 91 92 93
94 95 96 97 98 99 100

OVERALL VALUE: ★   ★★   ★★★   ★★★★   ★★★★★

TASTING NOTES

WINE:

VINTAGE: PRICE:

PRODUCER:

REGION & COUNTRY:

GRAPE VARIETY:

RECOMMENDED BY:

PLACE & DATE BOUGHT:

PLACE & DATE TASTED:

APPEARANCE:

NOSE:

TASTE:

FINISH:

OVERALL IMPRESSION:

OVERALL RATINGS: 70 71 72 73 74 75 76 77 78 79
80 81 82 83 84 85 86 87 88 89 90 91 92 93
94 95 96 97 98 99 100

OVERALL VALUE: ★   ★★   ★★★   ★★★★   ★★★★★

TASTING NOTES

WINE:

VINTAGE: PRICE:

PRODUCER:

REGION & COUNTRY:

GRAPE VARIETY:

RECOMMENDED BY:

PLACE & DATE BOUGHT:

PLACE & DATE TASTED:

APPEARANCE:

NOSE:

TASTE:

FINISH:

OVERALL IMPRESSION:

OVERALL RATINGS: 70 71 72 73 74 75 76 77 78 79
80 81 82 83 84 85 86 87 88 89 90 91 92 93
94 95 96 97 98 99 100

OVERALL VALUE: ★   ★★   ★★★   ★★★★   ★★★★★

TASTING NOTES

WINE:

VINTAGE: PRICE:

PRODUCER:

REGION & COUNTRY:

GRAPE VARIETY:

RECOMMENDED BY:

PLACE & DATE BOUGHT:

PLACE & DATE TASTED:

APPEARANCE:

NOSE:

TASTE:

FINISH:

OVERALL IMPRESSION:

OVERALL RATINGS: 70 71 72 73 74 75 76 77 78 79
80 81 82 83 84 85 86 87 88 89 90 91 92 93
94 95 96 97 98 99 100

OVERALL VALUE: ★   ★★   ★★★   ★★★★   ★★★★★

TASTING NOTES

WINE:

VINTAGE: PRICE:

PRODUCER:

REGION & COUNTRY:

GRAPE VARIETY:

RECOMMENDED BY:

PLACE & DATE BOUGHT:

PLACE & DATE TASTED:

APPEARANCE:

NOSE:

TASTE:

FINISH:

OVERALL IMPRESSION:

OVERALL RATINGS: 70 71 72 73 74 75 76 77 78 79
80 81 82 83 84 85 86 87 88 89 90 91 92 93
94 95 96 97 98 99 100

OVERALL VALUE: ★   ★★   ★★★   ★★★★   ★★★★★

TASTING NOTES

WINE:

VINTAGE: PRICE:

PRODUCER:

REGION & COUNTRY:

GRAPE VARIETY:

RECOMMENDED BY:

PLACE & DATE BOUGHT:

PLACE & DATE TASTED:

APPEARANCE:

NOSE:

TASTE:

FINISH:

OVERALL IMPRESSION:

OVERALL RATINGS: 70 71 72 73 74 **75** 76 77 78 79
80 81 82 83 84 85 86 87 88 89 90 91 92 93
94 95 96 97 98 99 100

OVERALL VALUE: ★   ★★   ★★★   ★★★★   ★★★★★

TASTING NOTES

WINE:

VINTAGE: PRICE:

PRODUCER:

REGION & COUNTRY:

GRAPE VARIETY:

RECOMMENDED BY:

PLACE & DATE BOUGHT:

PLACE & DATE TASTED:

APPEARANCE:

NOSE:

TASTE:

FINISH:

OVERALL IMPRESSION:

OVERALL RATINGS: 70 71 72 73 74 75 76 77 78 79
80 81 82 83 84 85 86 87 88 89 90 91 92 93
94 95 96 97 98 99 100

OVERALL VALUE: ★   ★★   ★★★   ★★★★   ★★★★★

TASTING NOTES

WINE:

VINTAGE: PRICE:

PRODUCER:

REGION & COUNTRY:

GRAPE VARIETY:

RECOMMENDED BY:

PLACE & DATE BOUGHT:

PLACE & DATE TASTED:

APPEARANCE:

NOSE:

TASTE:

FINISH:

OVERALL IMPRESSION:

OVERALL RATINGS: 70 71 72 73 74 75 76 77 78 79
80 81 82 83 84 85 86 87 88 89 90 91 92 93
94 95 96 97 98 99 100

OVERALL VALUE: ★   ★★   ★★★   ★★★★   ★★★★★

TASTING NOTES

WINE:

VINTAGE: PRICE:

PRODUCER:

REGION & COUNTRY:

GRAPE VARIETY:

RECOMMENDED BY:

PLACE & DATE BOUGHT:

PLACE & DATE TASTED:

APPEARANCE:

NOSE:

TASTE:

FINISH:

OVERALL IMPRESSION:

OVERALL RATINGS: 70 71 72 73 74 75 76 77 78 79
80 81 82 83 84 85 86 87 88 89 90 91 92 93
94 95 96 97 98 99 100

OVERALL VALUE: ★   ★★   ★★★   ★★★★   ★★★★★

TASTING NOTES

WINE:

VINTAGE: PRICE:

PRODUCER:

REGION & COUNTRY:

GRAPE VARIETY:

RECOMMENDED BY:

PLACE & DATE BOUGHT:

PLACE & DATE TASTED:

APPEARANCE:

NOSE:

TASTE:

FINISH:

OVERALL IMPRESSION:

OVERALL RATINGS: 70 71 72 73 74 75 76 77 78 79
80 81 82 83 84 85 86 87 88 89 90 91 92 93
94 95 96 97 98 99 100

OVERALL VALUE: ★   ★★   ★★★   ★★★★   ★★★★★

TASTING NOTES

WINE:

VINTAGE: PRICE:

PRODUCER:

REGION & COUNTRY:

GRAPE VARIETY:

RECOMMENDED BY:

PLACE & DATE BOUGHT:

PLACE & DATE TASTED:

APPEARANCE:

NOSE:

TASTE:

FINISH:

OVERALL IMPRESSION:

OVERALL RATINGS: 70 71 72 73 74 75 76 77 78 79
80 81 82 83 84 85 86 87 88 89 90 91 92 93
94 95 96 97 98 99 100

OVERALL VALUE: ★   ★★   ★★★   ★★★★   ★★★★★

TASTING NOTES

WINE:

VINTAGE: PRICE:

PRODUCER:

REGION & COUNTRY:

GRAPE VARIETY:

RECOMMENDED BY:

PLACE & DATE BOUGHT:

PLACE & DATE TASTED:

APPEARANCE:

NOSE:

TASTE:

FINISH:

OVERALL IMPRESSION:

OVERALL RATINGS: 70 71 72 73 74 75 76 77 78 79
80 81 82 83 84 85 86 87 88 89 90 91 92 93
94 95 96 97 98 99 100

OVERALL VALUE: ★   ★★   ★★★   ★★★★   ★★★★★

TASTING NOTES

WINE:

VINTAGE: PRICE:

PRODUCER:

REGION & COUNTRY:

GRAPE VARIETY:

RECOMMENDED BY:

PLACE & DATE BOUGHT:

PLACE & DATE TASTED:

APPEARANCE:

NOSE:

TASTE:

FINISH:

OVERALL IMPRESSION:

OVERALL RATINGS: 70 71 72 73 74 75 76 77 78 79
80 81 82 83 84 85 86 87 88 89 90 91 92 93
94 95 96 97 98 99 100

OVERALL VALUE: ★   ★★   ★★★   ★★★★   ★★★★★

TASTING NOTES

WINE:

VINTAGE: PRICE:

PRODUCER:

REGION & COUNTRY:

GRAPE VARIETY:

RECOMMENDED BY:

PLACE & DATE BOUGHT:

PLACE & DATE TASTED:

APPEARANCE:

NOSE:

TASTE:

FINISH:

OVERALL IMPRESSION:

OVERALL RATINGS: 70 71 72 73 74 75 76 77 78 79
80 81 82 83 84 85 86 87 88 89 90 91 92 93
94 95 96 97 98 99 100

OVERALL VALUE: ★   ★★   ★★★   ★★★★   ★★★★★

TASTING NOTES

WINE:

VINTAGE: PRICE:

PRODUCER:

REGION & COUNTRY:

GRAPE VARIETY:

RECOMMENDED BY:

PLACE & DATE BOUGHT:

PLACE & DATE TASTED:

APPEARANCE:

NOSE:

TASTE:

FINISH:

OVERALL IMPRESSION:

OVERALL RATINGS: 70 71 72 73 74 75 76 77 78 79
80 81 82 83 84 85 86 87 88 89 90 91 92 93
94 95 96 97 98 99 100

OVERALL VALUE: ★   ★★   ★★★   ★★★★   ★★★★★

TASTING NOTES

WINE:

VINTAGE: PRICE:

PRODUCER:

REGION & COUNTRY:

GRAPE VARIETY:

RECOMMENDED BY:

PLACE & DATE BOUGHT:

PLACE & DATE TASTED:

APPEARANCE:

NOSE:

TASTE:

FINISH:

OVERALL IMPRESSION:

OVERALL RATINGS: 70 71 72 73 74 75 76 77 78 79
80 81 82 83 84 85 86 87 88 89 90 91 92 93
94 95 96 97 98 99 100

OVERALL VALUE: ★   ★★   ★★★   ★★★★   ★★★★★

TASTING NOTES

WINE:

VINTAGE: PRICE:

PRODUCER:

REGION & COUNTRY:

GRAPE VARIETY:

RECOMMENDED BY:

PLACE & DATE BOUGHT:

PLACE & DATE TASTED:

APPEARANCE:

NOSE:

TASTE:

FINISH:

OVERALL IMPRESSION:

OVERALL RATINGS: 70 71 72 73 74 75 76 77 78 79
80 81 82 83 84 85 86 87 88 89 90 91 92 93
94 95 96 97 98 99 100

OVERALL VALUE: ★   ★★   ★★★   ★★★★   ★★★★★

TASTING NOTES

WINE:

VINTAGE: PRICE:

PRODUCER:

REGION & COUNTRY:

GRAPE VARIETY:

RECOMMENDED BY:

PLACE & DATE BOUGHT:

PLACE & DATE TASTED:

APPEARANCE:

NOSE:

TASTE:

FINISH:

OVERALL IMPRESSION:

OVERALL RATINGS: 70 71 72 73 74 75 76 77 78 79
80 81 82 83 84 85 86 87 88 89 90 91 92 93
94 95 96 97 98 99 100

OVERALL VALUE: ★   ★★   ★★★   ★★★★   ★★★★★

TASTING NOTES

WINE:

VINTAGE: PRICE:

PRODUCER:

REGION & COUNTRY:

GRAPE VARIETY:

RECOMMENDED BY:

PLACE & DATE BOUGHT:

PLACE & DATE TASTED:

APPEARANCE:

NOSE:

TASTE:

FINISH:

OVERALL IMPRESSION:

OVERALL RATINGS: 70 71 72 73 74 75 76 77 78 79
80 81 82 83 84 85 86 87 88 89 90 91 92 93
94 95 96 97 98 99 100

OVERALL VALUE: ★   ★★   ★★★   ★★★★   ★★★★★

TASTING NOTES

WINE:

VINTAGE: PRICE:

PRODUCER:

REGION & COUNTRY:

GRAPE VARIETY:

RECOMMENDED BY:

PLACE & DATE BOUGHT:

PLACE & DATE TASTED:

APPEARANCE:

NOSE:

TASTE:

FINISH:

OVERALL IMPRESSION:

OVERALL RATINGS: 70 71 72 73 74 75 76 77 78 79
80 81 82 83 84 85 86 87 88 89 90 91 92 93
94 95 96 97 98 99 100

OVERALL VALUE: ★   ★★   ★★★   ★★★★   ★★★★★

TASTING NOTES

WINE:

VINTAGE: PRICE:

PRODUCER:

REGION & COUNTRY:

GRAPE VARIETY:

RECOMMENDED BY:

PLACE & DATE BOUGHT:

PLACE & DATE TASTED:

APPEARANCE:

NOSE:

TASTE:

FINISH:

OVERALL IMPRESSION:

OVERALL RATINGS: 70 71 72 73 74 75 76 77 78 79
80 81 82 83 84 85 86 87 88 89 90 91 92 93
94 95 96 97 98 99 100

OVERALL VALUE: ★   ★★   ★★★   ★★★★   ★★★★★

TASTING NOTES

WINE:

VINTAGE: PRICE:

PRODUCER:

REGION & COUNTRY:

GRAPE VARIETY:

RECOMMENDED BY:

PLACE & DATE BOUGHT:

PLACE & DATE TASTED:

APPEARANCE:

NOSE:

TASTE:

FINISH:

OVERALL IMPRESSION:

OVERALL RATINGS: 70 71 72 73 74 75 76 77 78 79
80 81 82 83 84 85 86 87 88 89 90 91 92 93
94 95 96 97 98 99 100

OVERALL VALUE: ★   ★★   ★★★   ★★★★   ★★★★★

TASTING NOTES

WINE:

VINTAGE: PRICE:

PRODUCER:

REGION & COUNTRY:

GRAPE VARIETY:

RECOMMENDED BY:

PLACE & DATE BOUGHT:

PLACE & DATE TASTED:

APPEARANCE:

NOSE:

TASTE:

FINISH:

OVERALL IMPRESSION:

OVERALL RATINGS: 70 71 72 73 74 75 76 77 78 79
80 81 82 83 84 85 86 87 88 89 90 91 92 93
94 95 96 97 98 99 100

OVERALL VALUE: ★   ★★   ★★★   ★★★★   ★★★★★

TASTING NOTES

WINE:

VINTAGE: PRICE:

PRODUCER:

REGION & COUNTRY:

GRAPE VARIETY:

RECOMMENDED BY:

PLACE & DATE BOUGHT:

PLACE & DATE TASTED:

APPEARANCE:

NOSE:

TASTE:

FINISH:

OVERALL IMPRESSION:

OVERALL RATINGS: 70 71 72 73 74 75 76 77 78 79
80 81 82 83 84 85 86 87 88 89 90 91 92 93
94 95 96 97 98 99 100

OVERALL VALUE: ★   ★★   ★★★   ★★★★   ★★★★★

TASTING NOTES

WINE:

VINTAGE: PRICE:

PRODUCER:

REGION & COUNTRY:

GRAPE VARIETY:

RECOMMENDED BY:

PLACE & DATE BOUGHT:

PLACE & DATE TASTED:

APPEARANCE:

NOSE:

TASTE:

FINISH:

OVERALL IMPRESSION:

OVERALL RATINGS: 70 71 72 73 74 75 76 77 78 79
80 81 82 83 84 85 86 87 88 89 90 91 92 93
94 95 96 97 98 99 100

OVERALL VALUE: ★   ★★   ★★★   ★★★★   ★★★★★

*Wine in itself is
an excellent thing.*

Pope Pius XII

*A meal without wine
is like a day
without sunshine.*

Louis Vaudable

Tasting Notes

WINE:

VINTAGE: PRICE:

PRODUCER:

REGION & COUNTRY:

GRAPE VARIETY:

RECOMMENDED BY:

PLACE & DATE BOUGHT:

PLACE & DATE TASTED:

APPEARANCE:

NOSE:

TASTE:

FINISH:

OVERALL IMPRESSION:

OVERALL RATINGS: 70 71 72 73 74 75 76 77 78 79
80 81 82 83 84 85 86 87 88 89 90 91 92 93
94 95 96 97 98 99 100

OVERALL VALUE: ★   ★★   ★★★   ★★★★   ★★★★★

TASTING NOTES

WINE:

VINTAGE: PRICE:

PRODUCER:

REGION & COUNTRY:

GRAPE VARIETY:

RECOMMENDED BY:

PLACE & DATE BOUGHT:

PLACE & DATE TASTED:

APPEARANCE:

NOSE:

TASTE:

FINISH:

OVERALL IMPRESSION:

OVERALL RATINGS: 70 71 72 73 74 75 76 77 78 79
80 81 82 83 84 85 86 87 88 89 90 91 92 93
94 95 96 97 98 99 100

OVERALL VALUE: ★   ★★   ★★★   ★★★★   ★★★★★

TASTING NOTES

WINE:

VINTAGE: PRICE:

PRODUCER:

REGION & COUNTRY:

GRAPE VARIETY:

RECOMMENDED BY:

PLACE & DATE BOUGHT:

PLACE & DATE TASTED:

APPEARANCE:

NOSE:

TASTE:

FINISH:

OVERALL IMPRESSION:

OVERALL RATINGS: 70 71 72 73 74 75 76 77 78 79
80 81 82 83 84 85 86 87 88 89 90 91 92 93
94 95 96 97 98 99 100

OVERALL VALUE: ★   ★★   ★★★   ★★★★   ★★★★★

TASTING NOTES

WINE:

VINTAGE: PRICE:

PRODUCER:

REGION & COUNTRY:

GRAPE VARIETY:

RECOMMENDED BY:

PLACE & DATE BOUGHT:

PLACE & DATE TASTED:

APPEARANCE:

NOSE:

TASTE:

FINISH:

OVERALL IMPRESSION:

OVERALL RATINGS: 70 71 72 73 74 75 76 77 78 79
80 81 82 83 84 85 86 87 88 89 90 91 92 93
94 95 96 97 98 99 100

OVERALL VALUE: ★ ★★ ★★★ ★★★★ ★★★★★

TASTING NOTES

WINE:

VINTAGE: PRICE:

PRODUCER:

REGION & COUNTRY:

GRAPE VARIETY:

RECOMMENDED BY:

PLACE & DATE BOUGHT:

PLACE & DATE TASTED:

APPEARANCE:

NOSE:

TASTE:

FINISH:

OVERALL IMPRESSION:

OVERALL RATINGS: 70 71 72 73 74 75 76 77 78 79
80 81 82 83 84 85 86 87 88 89 90 91 92 93
94 95 96 97 98 99 100

OVERALL VALUE: ★   ★★   ★★★   ★★★★   ★★★★★

Tasting Notes

WINE:

VINTAGE: PRICE:

PRODUCER:

REGION & COUNTRY:

GRAPE VARIETY:

RECOMMENDED BY:

PLACE & DATE BOUGHT:

PLACE & DATE TASTED:

APPEARANCE:

NOSE:

TASTE:

FINISH:

OVERALL IMPRESSION:

OVERALL RATINGS: 70 71 72 73 74 75 76 77 78 79
80 81 82 83 84 85 86 87 88 89 90 91 92 93
94 95 96 97 98 99 100

OVERALL VALUE: ★   ★★   ★★★   ★★★★   ★★★★★

glossary

Although wine is clearly much more than mere lubrication, to appreciate it, all you need is an interest and a sense of smell.

Jancis Robinson

GLOSSARY

ACIDITY: Essential component in wine affected mostly by tartaric acid naturally found in grapes. Low acid wines will be "smooth" and "round," but with too little acid, a wine can taste flat and dull. High acid wines feel "crisp" and "vivacious," but too much acidity can make them sour and unpleasant.

ALCOHOL: A colorless liquid by-product of the fermentation process that contributes to a wine's body and overall flavor. The alcohol level for most red wines falls between 11 and 14 percent, and for white wines, between 9 and 14 percent.

APPELLATION: The official name of the geographic location for growing grapes, usually found on a wine's label and often part of its name.

AROMA: The individual smells or flavors of a wine that include, among other categories, fruits, spices, flowers, and earth.

BALANCE: The combination of acidity, sweetness, tannins, and alcohol in a wine. Quality wines are well-balanced, with no one component dominating the others.

BODY: The impression of weight and size of a wine, usually described as light, medium, or full.

Full-bodied wines feel bigger and heavier in the mouth.

BOUQUET: Refers to the multi-layered combination of smells or flavors in a wine.

COMPLEXITY: The depth of a wine, made of many different aromas and flavors.

CRISP: Pleasantly acidic.

DECANT: To transfer wine from a bottle into a container or glasses to allow it to aerate or breathe. Aerating younger wines may soften harsh flavors, while decanting older red wines allows for sediment to be poured off and any unpleasant odors to be released.

DEPTH: The multi-dimensional flavors of a fine wine.

FERMENTATION: The natural process by which yeast transforms the sugars in grape juice to create alcohol, or wine.

FINISH: The aftertaste, or final impression, of a wine after it has been swallowed or spat.

FIRM: Pleasantly tannic.

FLABBY: Not acidic enough.

FRESH: Pleasantly acidic.

HARD: Too tannic or bitter.

HOLLOW or LEAN: Not fruity enough.

HOT: Describes a wine with too much alcohol.

LEES: Sediment composed of grape solids and yeast cells that forms at the bottom of a barrel or vat following fermentation.

LEGS: The dripping lines, or tears, wine forms after it has been swirled inside a glass.

LENGTH: One of the first indicators of high quality. "Long" describes a wine that can be tasted fully during the first sip, all across the tongue. A "short" wine may start with a bang but lose its taste almost immediately.

MATURE: Sufficiently aged.

MOUTHFEEL: The texture of a wine as sensed by the mouth and tongue.

PALATE: The flavor or taste of a wine.

ROUND: Having good body and not too much tannin.

SOMMELIER: French name for a wine expert. In some restaurants, the sommelier assists customers with wine selection, presentation, and service.

TANNIN: Substance found in grape seeds and stems that serves as a natural preservative in wine. Tannin dries the mouth, leaving a puckery after-taste that lends a smooth, mellow flavor to aged wines or a rough, harsh taste to young red wines. When well matched by the other elements, tannin contributes to the backbone and structure of a good red wine. Cabernet Sauvignon and other full-flavored reds contain high amounts of tannins.

TASTEVIN: This word, generally reserved for connoisseurs and sommeliers (literally, "taste wine"), refers to the small silver cup first used for tasting wine in underground wine cellars. The round depressions that decorate the cup reflect the candlelight, allowing the wine to be seen in near-darkness.

VARIETAL: Refers to the variety or type of grape used to make a wine.

VINTAGE: The year grapes were harvested to make a wine.

VISCOSITY: The body or thickness of a wine, usually used when discussing wines that have high sugar or alcohol content.

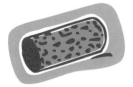